Whales and
Dolphins

KINGFISHER

Published in 2010 by Kingfisher
an imprint of Macmillan Children's Books
a division of Macmillan Publishers Limited
20 New Wharf Road
London N1 9RR
Basingstoke and Oxford
Associated companies throughout the world
www.panmacmillan.com

ISBN 978-0-7534-3000-2

First published as *Kingfisher Young Knowledge: Whales and Dolphins* in 2005
Additional material produced for Macmillan Children's Books by Discovery Books Ltd

Copyright © Macmillan Children's Books 2010

1 3 5 7 9 8 6 4 2

1TR/0410/WKT/UNTD/140MA/C

A CIP catalogue record for this book is available from the British Library.

Printed in China

Note to readers: the website addresses listed in this book are correct at
the time of going to print. However, due to the ever-changing nature
of the internet, website addresses and content can change. Websites
can contain links that are unsuitable for children. The publisher cannot
be held responsible for changes in website addresses or content, or
for information obtained through a third party. We strongly advise
that internet searches should be supervised by an adult.

Acknowledgements

The publishers would like to thank the following for permission to reproduce their material. Every care has been taken
to trace copyright holders. However, if there have been unintentional omissions or failure to trace copyright holders,
we apologize and will, if informed, endeavour to make corrections in any future edition.
b = bottom, *c* = centre, *l* = left, *t* = top, *r* = right

Cover main Shutterstock/Kristian Skeulic; cover *l* Seapics/Masa Ushioda; cover *r* Seapics/James D. Watt; 1 Seapics/Masa Ushioda; 2–3 Getty/Taxi; 4–5 Nature pl/Brandon Cole; 6
Minden/Flip Nicklin; 7*t* Seapics/Armin Maywald; 7*b* Seapics/Doug Perrine; 8–9 Seapics/Doug Perrine; 8*b* Nature pl/Sue Flood; 9*b* Seapics/Ingrid Visser; 10 Minden/Flip Nicklin;
11*t* Seapics/David B Fleetham; 11*c* Seapics/Mark Conlin; 11*b* OSF/David Fleetham; 12*b* Seapics/Michael S Nolan; 13*t* Minden/Mitsuaki Iwago; 14–15 Corbis/Craig Tuttle; 15*t*
Seapics/Doug Perrine; 15*r* Corbis/Lester V Bergman; 15*b* Seapics/Doug Perrine; 16–17 Alamy; 17*t* Seapics/Hiroya Minakuchi; 17*b* Seapics/Masa Ushioda; 18–19 Seapics/Duncan
Murrell; 19*t* Seapics/Philip Colla; 20–21 Minden/Flip Nicklin; 20*b* Ardea; 22–23 SeaQuest; 23*b* Seapics; 24–25 Minden Flip Nicklin; 25*t* Seapics/Masa Ushioda; 25*b* Seapics Xavier
Safont; 26*b* Seapics Hiroya Minakuchi; 26–27 Seapics Masa Ushioda; 27*t* Seapics Robert L Pitman; 28*b* Seapics/James D Watt; 29*t* Seapics/Bob Cranston; 30–31 Seapics/Doug
Perrine; 31*t* Seapics/James D Watt; 31*b* Seapics/Masa Ushioda; 32–33 Seapic; 32*b* Seapics/Hiroya Minakuchi; 33*t* Seapics/John KB Ford; 34 Minden/Flip Nicklin; 35*t* Corbis;
35*b* AA; 36–37 SeaQuest; 36*c* Corbis/Peter Turnley; 38–39 Seapics/Phillip Colla; 39*t* Minden/Flip Nicklin; 39*b* Minden/Flip Nicklin; 40–41 Minden/Mike Parry; 41 Corbis; 48*t*
Shutterstock Images/Lars Christensen; 48*b* Shutterstock Images/CampCrazy Photography; 49*t* Shutterstock Images/Ivan Cholakov Gostock-dot-net; 49*b* Shutterstock Images/
J Helgason; 52*c* Shutterstock Images/Kristian Sekulic; 52*b* Shutterstock Images/rm; 53*t* Shutterstock Images/Karel Gallas; 56*b* Shutterstock Images/Steve Noakes

Illustrations: 12–13 Michael Langham Rowe; 23*t*, 28–29 Steve Weston
Commissioned photography on pages 42–47 by Andy Crawford. Thank you to models Lewis Manu, Adam Dyer and Rebecca Roper

Whales and Dolphins

Caroline Harris

KINGFISHER

Contents

What are whales and dolphins?

Whales and dolphins are mammals that live in water. They have warm blood and swim to the ocean's surface to breathe.

Baby care

A dolphin mother usually gives birth to one baby at a time, called a calf. The newborn calf swims close to its mother's side for the first few weeks.

Bristly faces

Most mammals are covered with hair or fur. This porpoise's skin is smooth, but young cetaceans (the name that scientists use for whales, dolphins and porpoises) still have hairs on their faces.

Grand old age

Dolphins can live for up to 50 years, while large whales such as this southern right whale may live to be 100!

All around the world

There are more than 80 types of whale, dolphin and porpoise. They live all over the world – in freezing oceans, tropical seas and even in rivers.

Icy white
The beluga is also called the white whale. It makes its home in the very cold Arctic seas around Canada, Alaska and Russia.

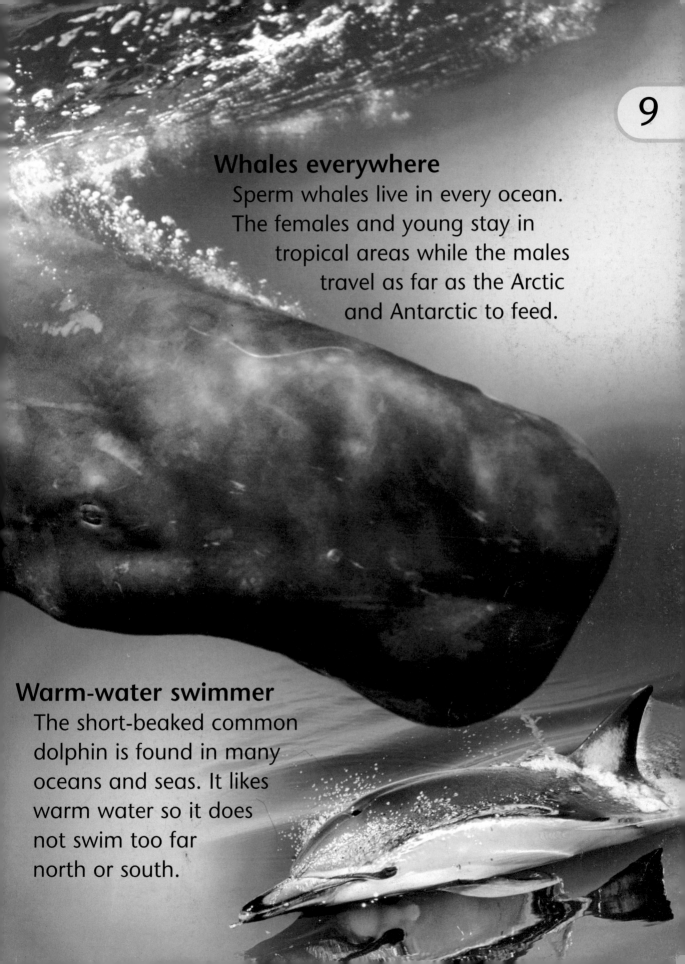

Whales everywhere

Sperm whales live in every ocean. The females and young stay in tropical areas while the males travel as far as the Arctic and Antarctic to feed.

Warm-water swimmer

The short-beaked common dolphin is found in many oceans and seas. It likes warm water so it does not swim too far north or south.

Amazing creatures

Whales and dolphins come in some incredible shapes and sizes. Did you know that the largest animal on earth is a whale?

Dolphin magic

The boto, or Amazon river dolphin, is one of four species of dolphin that are found only in rivers. It is also called the pink dolphin because it has rose-coloured skin.

Sea giant

The blue whale is the world's largest mammal. It can weigh 190 tonnes – the same as 32 elephants. A blue whale this huge has a heart the size of a car!

blue whale

skeleton of a blue whale

Water unicorn

The male narwhal has a tusk that can reach three metres long. Tales of unicorns may have begun when people first saw narwhal tusks.

Ancient whales

When the dinosaurs died out, mammals began to live in many different places. This is how whales and dolphins came to live in the oceans.

Digging up the past

We know about ancient cetaceans through the fossils and bones they left behind, such as this dolphin skull.

Grass-eating cousins

Cows, sheep, whales
and dolphins share
the same ancestor –
an ancient mammal
that lived on land
and ate leaves.

Early whale

Basilosaurus lived
40 million years ago. Over
a long time, the land mammals
that moved into the sea changed
their shape to suit life in the water.

Built for the sea

The smooth, long shape of cetaceans means they are able to swim through water easily. Salty seawater is good at keeping heavy things buoyant, which is why whales can grow very large.

Full power

Instead of back legs, cetaceans have immensely strong tails with two flat paddles called flukes. Bottlenose dolphins can stand up using their tails alone.

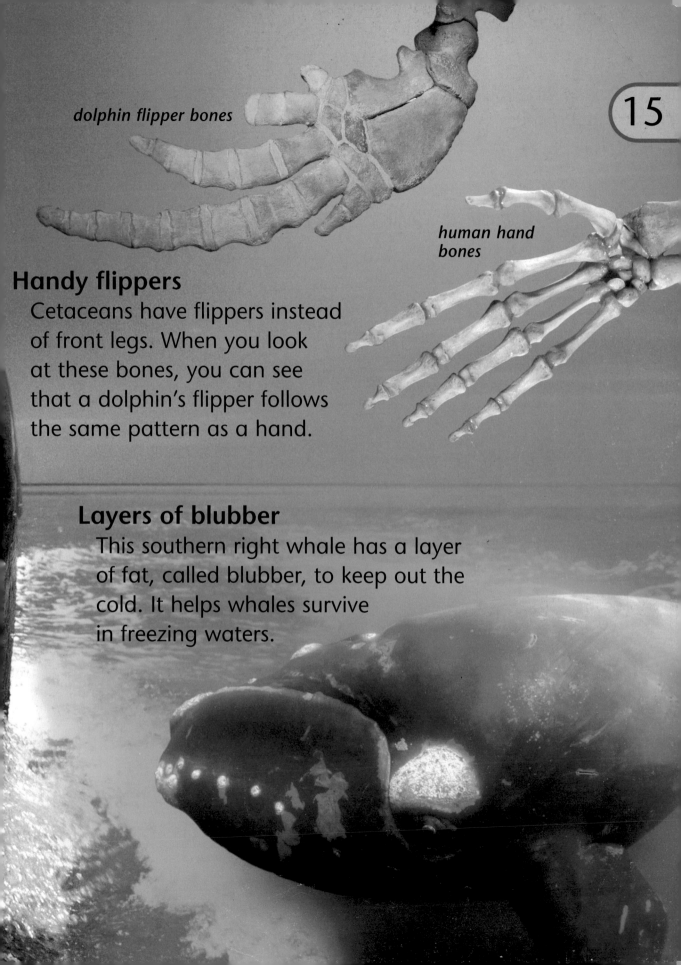

dolphin flipper bones

human hand bones

Handy flippers

Cetaceans have flippers instead of front legs. When you look at these bones, you can see that a dolphin's flipper follows the same pattern as a hand.

Layers of blubber

This southern right whale has a layer of fat, called blubber, to keep out the cold. It helps whales survive in freezing waters.

Coming up **for air**

Like other mammals, whales and dolphins breathe using their lungs. This means coming to the surface to take in fresh air and blow out used air.

Deep down

Most whales can stay underwater for half an hour before needing to take a breath. Cetaceans take in air through a blowhole in the top of their head.

Blowing high

Many whales, such as this blue whale, have a double blowhole. The blowhole closes up when they dive so water will not get in.

No one the same

Dolphins have a single blowhole. The pattern of mist, called 'blow', that sprays out is different for every species of cetacean.

Filter feeders

Cetaceans are split into two groups: those that have teeth and those that do not. The toothless whales, known as baleen whales, include humpbacks and greys. They feed by filtering tiny marine animals and small fish from the sea.

What is baleen?

Instead of teeth, toothless whales have baleen – stiff, hairy sheets that hang in rows from their top jaws. Baleen traps food as water is filtered through it.

Big eaters

To eat enough, humpbacks gulp vast mouthfuls of water. Folds in their necks expand like a balloon to let in even more.

Clever hunters

All dolphins and porpoises and more than half of whale species have teeth. They eat fish and larger sea creatures. Sperm whales love to eat giant squid.

Fearless predators

The orca, often called the killer whale, is in fact a large dolphin. Its diet includes sealions and even other cetaceans.

Open wide

A dolphin's teeth are used for grabbing, not chewing. They swallow their prey whole.

Team work

Bottlenose dolphins often hunt together. They surround groups of fish, sometimes driving them onto land and coming halfway out of the water to grab them.

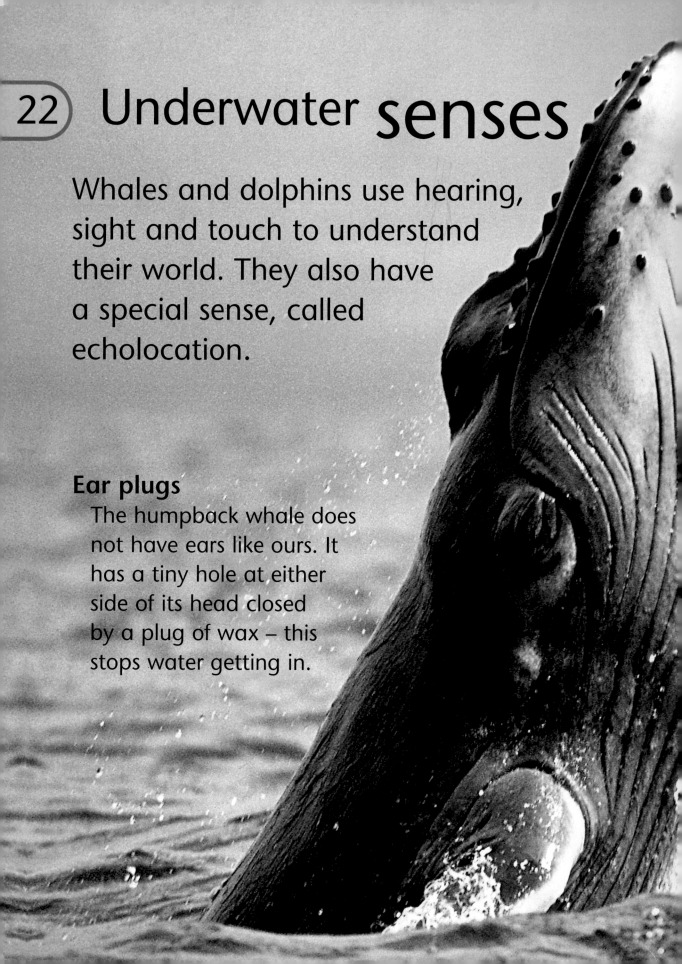

Underwater senses

Whales and dolphins use hearing, sight and touch to understand their world. They also have a special sense, called echolocation.

Ear plugs

The humpback whale does not have ears like ours. It has a tiny hole at either side of its head closed by a plug of wax – this stops water getting in.

What is echolocation?

Echolocation is used by dolphins to navigate and find prey. They make clicking noises that 'bounce', or echo, off an object, telling them where it is and what it is like.

Clear vision

They may have only small eyes, but most cetaceans see well. A thick, greasy liquid stops the eyes becoming sore in the salty water.

Sea songs

All cetaceans use sounds to communicate. Baleen whales make low sounds, from loud grunts and squeals to bubbling noises. Dolphins whistle, squeak and click.

Noisy neighbours

Dolphins make different noises for different reasons. Opening and shutting their mouths, called jaw-clapping, is a sign there may be a fight on the way.

The latest tune
Male humpbacks sing patterns of notes and sounds that can last up to half an hour.

Brain power
Dolphins have large brains for the size of their bodies. They are fast learners and can even understand simple sentences.

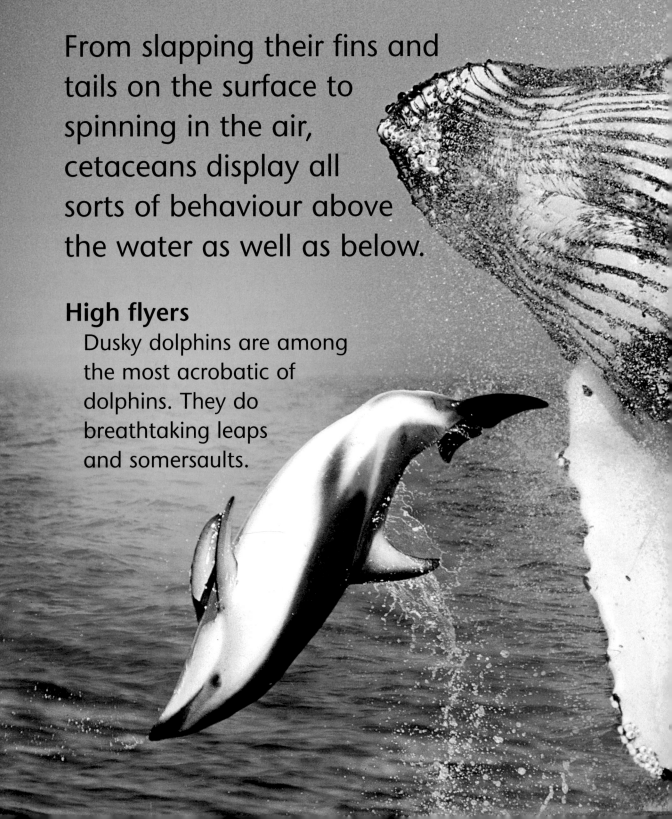

Playing with **waves**

From slapping their fins and tails on the surface to spinning in the air, cetaceans display all sorts of behaviour above the water as well as below.

High flyers

Dusky dolphins are among the most acrobatic of dolphins. They do breathtaking leaps and somersaults.

Who's there?

Orcas spyhop, sticking
their heads straight
up out of the water,
to spot penguins
and seals on the ice.

A grand sight

When whales
launch themselves out
of the sea, it is called
breaching. Humpbacks have
been seen breaching 100
times, over and over again.

Moving home

Whales travel, or migrate, between cold seas in summer, where there is plenty of food, and warmer waters in winter, where they have their families.

Record holders

Humpbacks and greys make the longest journeys. They can swim up to 16,000 kilometres in a year.

North America

South America

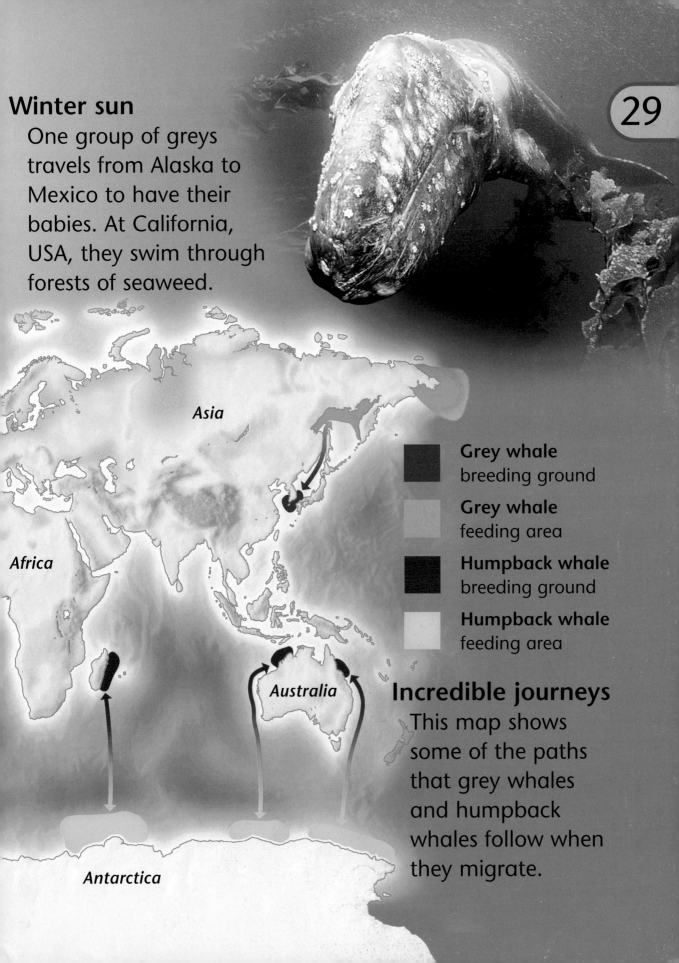

Winter sun

One group of greys travels from Alaska to Mexico to have their babies. At California, USA, they swim through forests of seaweed.

Asia

Africa

Grey whale breeding ground

Grey whale feeding area

Humpback whale breeding ground

Humpback whale feeding area

Australia

Incredible journeys

This map shows some of the paths that grey whales and humpback whales follow when they migrate.

Antarctica

New lives

Whale and dolphin babies swim as soon as they are born, but it takes many years until a calf is an adult.

Big babies

A humpback calf can measure a third of its mother's length when born! It will feed on her milk for the first 11 months.

Long pregnancy

Dolphins can be pregnant
for more than a year. The
actual birth, though,
is quick and may
be over in less
than an hour.

Keeping close

Cetacean mothers stay
close to their calves so
they can protect them
from predators.

Social animals

A group of cetaceans is known as a pod. Many pods are related, while others come together to feed or to protect young.

Family ties

All the members of an orca pod are related to one original mother or grandmother. Orcas usually stay with their family for life.

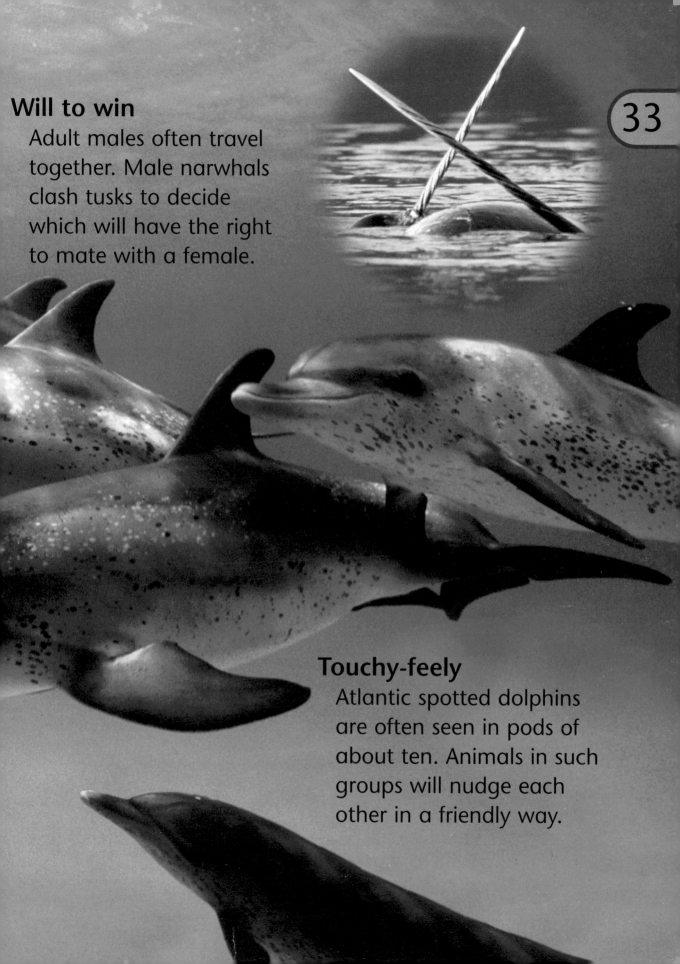

Will to win

Adult males often travel together. Male narwhals clash tusks to decide which will have the right to mate with a female.

Touchy-feely

Atlantic spotted dolphins are often seen in pods of about ten. Animals in such groups will nudge each other in a friendly way.

Making friends

People have always seen dolphins as friendly creatures. Whales were once thought of as monsters, but today we want to protect them.

Watery friends

Swimming with dolphins has become popular with adults and children. Dolphins will even help people who are in trouble in the sea.

Ancient links

This painting of dolphins is on a wall at the Palace of Knossos on the Greek island of Crete. It is 3,500 years old.

Big books

There are many stories about giant whales. In the Bible, Jonah was swallowed by a whale – and survived.

Human dangers

Some things people do harm cetaceans. For a long time, whales have been hunted for their meat, baleen and blubber. Fishing nets and pollution are added dangers.

Whale rescue

Many dolphins and whales get caught and can die in fishing nets. This tangled-up sperm whale is being freed by a diver.

Under threat

The Yangtze River, China, is home to the baiji. This dolphin is endangered because the river is full of pollution.

Whaling ban

Whale hunting – known
as whaling – has killed
millions of cetaceans.
Most countries
have agreed to
stop completely.

Growing knowledge

The more we discover about whales and dolphins, the more amazing we find they are. It is important to know as much as we can about them so that they can be better protected.

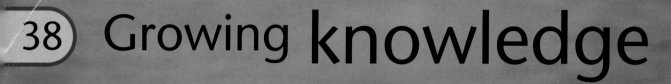

Getting to know them

Researchers can identify individual Risso's dolphins from the scars on their bodies. The pattern on each dolphin's body is different.

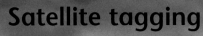

Satellite tagging

Cetaceans can now be followed from space! The tag on this beluga sends information to a satellite, which can then track where the beluga is.

Looking and learning

There are chances to watch whales, dolphins and porpoises in the wild throughout the world, from Ireland to the Caribbean and Canada to Australia.

Free to roam
Today, there are a few cetacean sanctuaries. It is hoped that in the future there will be more.

Near the shore

Many species, especially of dolphins, come close to the coast. All you need to spot them is a pair of binoculars – and some patience.

Thrilling sight

Special boat tours can give a great view. Responsible tours do not crowd the animals and make sure they are not disturbed.

Dolphin mobile

Leaping high

Hang this mobile in your bedroom and you will have dolphins dancing before your eyes. Shiny paper makes them sparkle in the light.

You will need
- Pencil
- Tracing paper
- Thin cardboard
- Scissors
- Moulding dough
- Compass
- Foil/shiny paper
- Glue
- Ruler
- Ribbon
- Thick cardboard (30cm x 30cm)

dolphin template

Decorate each dolphin with foil or shiny paper

Trace the template and transfer the shape onto thin cardboard. Do this five times so you have five dolphins. Cut out the dolphins.

Place moulding dough under the top fin of each dolphin shape. Using a compass, make a hole in each fin as shown.

3

Draw a line from the bottom-left corner of the thick cardboard to the top-right corner using a ruler. Cut along the line to make two triangles and decorate them.

4

Cut a notch halfway down the peak of one triangle. Cut a notch halfway up from the bottom of the other triangle. Make holes at the ends of each triangle.

5

Slot the triangles together to form the hanger. Make a hole where the two triangles meet at the bottom and another at the top.

Use ribbon to attach each dolphin to the hanger and fasten the knots. Pull ribbon through the hole at the top of the hanger to make a loop. You can now hang up your mobile.

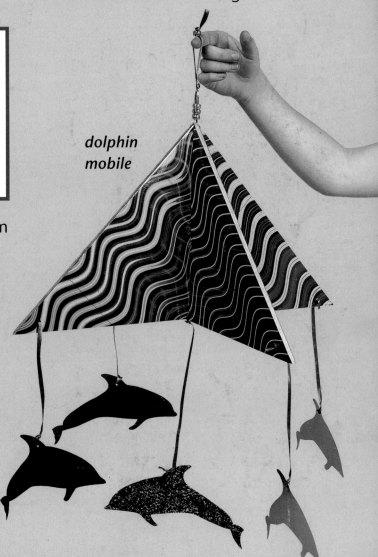

dolphin mobile

Whale bookmark

Intelligent creatures

Cetaceans are among the smartest animals. Make markers in the shape of sea mammals to keep your place in favourite books.

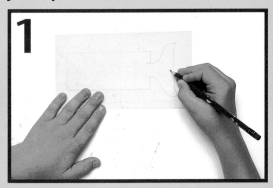

1

Measure a rectangle 6cm x 15cm. Draw a whale's tail at one short end of the shape. Draw waves where the tail meets the sea.

You will need
- Card
- Ruler
- Pencil
- Scissors
- Blue holographic paper
- Glue
- Felt-tip pens
- Glitter pens

2

Cut out the bookmark, being careful to cut around the shape of the whale's tail and around the top of the waves.

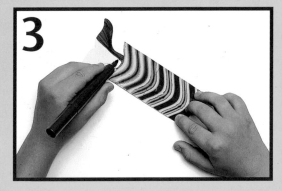

3

Glue blue holographic paper to both sides of the bookmark for the sea. Use felt-tip pens and glitter pens to colour in the tail.

Does it float?

Testing buoyancy

When you put different items in the water, some float on the surface and others sink to the bottom. Whales and dolphins need to come up for air, so they have to be buoyant enough not to sink straight down.

You will need
- Large clear bowl
- Water
- Apple
- Pebble
- Cork
- Ice cube

1

Think about the apple, pebble, cork and ice cube. Will they float or will they sink?

2 One by one, put each item into a bowl of water – were you right about which would float and which would sink?

Blue whale poster

Sea giants

Blue whales are the biggest animals on earth. They can reach 33 metres long, which is the size of a large swimming pool. This project will give you an idea of how large they are.

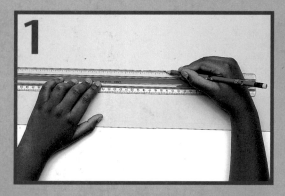

1

Using a ruler, measure and mark a 30cm space, then a 2cm space, an 8cm space, another 2cm space and, finally, a 6cm space.

You will need
- A1 card (66cm x 30cm)
- Ruler
- Pencil
- Paints
- Paintbrush
- Tissue paper: green, blue, red
- Glue
- Cotton wool
- Scissors
- Gold holographic paper

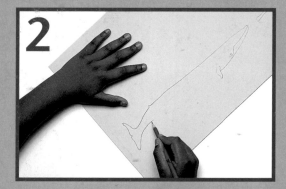

2

Draw a blue whale from tail to head in the 30cm space. Then draw an orca in the 8cm space and an elephant in the 6cm space.

3

Paint the blue whale, orca and elephant, copying the colours and markings shown on the final picture on the opposite page.

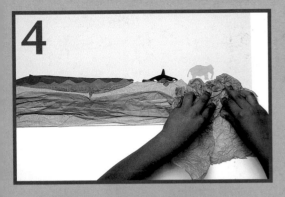

4

Decorate the picture with strips of tissue paper: green for land under the elephant and blue for the sea around the orca and whale.

5

Glue down cotton wool clouds. Then cut out a circle and 8 strips of gold holographic paper, and glue them down to make a sun.

To finish your picture, twist some red tissue paper and glue it down to create a border. Now you can see how large a blue whale is!

Glossary

Acrobatic – making movements that are difficult and skilful

Ancestor – an animal from which later animals have developed

Ancient – very old

Baleen – the thin, hairy plates in a whale's mouth

Behaviour – how animals act

Binoculars – an instrument with lenses for both eyes, which you can use in order to see objects that are far away

Blowhole – the airway that whales, dolphins and porpoises breathe through

Brain – the body part inside the head that is used to learn and think

Breeding ground – the place where animals go to find a mate and have their young

Buoyant – able to float in water

Calf – a baby dolphin or whale

Cetacean – the group name for whales, dolphins and porpoises

Coast – where the land meets the sea

Communicate – to send a message to another creature

Dive – to drop down head first

Endangered – in danger of dying out

Expand – to increase in size

Fat – the soft, oily part under the skin of an animal

Filtering – collecting tiny objects from the liquid (such as water) they are floating in

Fossil – evidence of a living thing from the past that is preserved in rock

Identify – to recognize or name

Journey – a long trip from one place to another

Lungs – the parts inside the body used for breathing

Mammal – a warm-blooded animal that feeds its young milk

Marine – from the sea

Navigate – to find your way

Patience – the ability to wait for a long time for something to happen

Pattern – if things are in a pattern then they are put together in a similar way

Pollution – harmful waste

Popular – liked by a lot of people

Predator – an animal that hunts and eats other animals

Pregnancy – the time when a baby grows inside its mother

Prey – an animal that gets eaten by other animals

Protect – to prevent something or someone from harm

Related – being part of the same family

Responsible – a responsible person behaves properly, without having to be supervised

Sanctuary – a safe place, protected from harm by humans

Satellite – a spacecraft that orbits the Earth

Scar – a mark left on the skin after a cut has healed

Social – living in a group

Somersault – a forwards or backwards roll where the body is brought over the head

Species – a set of animals or plants with the same features

Squid – a sea creature with a long, soft body and lots of tentacles

Tropical – an area near the equator where it is always hot

Unicorn – a mythical animal like a horse with a long horn

Wax – an oily material in the ear that protects it

This book includes material that would be particularly useful in helping to teach children aged 7–11. It covers many elements of the English and Science curricula and provides opportunities for cross-curricular lessons, especially those involving Geography and Art.

Extension activities:

Writing

Each double-page information spread has a title, introduction and three paragraphs of text, each with its own sub-heading.

1) Choose any creature in this book and write a report on it using this structure.

2) On pages 12–13 and 14–15 you will find information on animal bodies. Make up a creature suited to marine living. Write an explanation of how its characteristics allow it to survive in water.

Speaking and listening

1) Prepare for a class debate on the rights and wrongs of hunting whales.

2) Investigate other human threats to sea creatures (eg tuna fishing) and prepare a one-minute presentation on them.

Science

The topic of whales and dolphins relates to the scientific themes of growth (pp6–7, 30–31); types and characteristics of animals (pp8–9, 12–13, 16–17, 18–19); habitats (pp14, 28–29); skeletons (p15); insulation (p15); interdependence (pp32–33, 34, 36–37, 40–41); separating materials (pp18–19); diet (p20); teeth (p21); senses (pp22–23); sound (pp23, 24–25); forces (pp26–27 – how do whales launch themselves from the sea?)

1) Which melts faster, freshwater ice or salty ice? Devise an experiment to find out.

2) Sea water evaporates and falls on us as rain. So why isn't rain salty? Devise an experiment to find out.

Cross-curricular links

1) *History and Science:* Fossils are evidence of life in the past, such as dinosaurs. Discuss what they can and can't tell us.

2) *Geography:* Investigate great sea migrations and plot them on a world map.

3) *Art and Literacy:* Why did people paint on walls? Discuss. Design a painting for the wall of a classroom, or a bedroom. How are they different?

4) *Geography:* environmental issues. What is pollution and how is it affecting sea animals? How might this, in turn, affect us?

Using the projects

Children can follow or adapt these projects at home. Here are some ideas for extending them:

Pages 42–43: Make a mobile using only recycled materials such as packaging.

Page 44: Experiment to find other materials for the bookmark. Can you sew part of it?

Page 45: Test the buoyancy of pumice stone, sandstone, granite and a small brick.

Page 46: Add moving parts to the whale picture using levers and slides or an air pump. Make the picture in three dimensions.

Did you know?

- Dolphins can swim up to 260 metres below the surface of the ocean.

- Dolphins can stay underwater for up to 15 minutes. The sperm whale can stay underwater for as long as 90 minutes.

- The largest dolphin is the orca, also known as the 'killer whale'.

- A bottlenose dolphin's brain weighs between 1,500 and 1,600 grams. That's the same as one and a half bags of sugar.

- The blue whale is the largest animal in the world.

- Male whales use their singing voices to try and attract females during the mating season.

- Whales breathe air like we do. They need to reach the surface of the ocean in order to take in air through a blowhole.

- Whales can swim as fast as 48 kilometres per hour. The fastest human sprinter can run at 36 kilometres per hour.

- Whales and dolphins do not sleep like we do. They only rest half of their brain at a time. The other half continues to operate. Otherwise they would stop breathing and drown.

- Male dolphins are called bulls and female dolphins are called cows.

- Scientists have discovered that dolphins are as clever as human toddlers. They are capable of recognizing their own reflection in the mirror.

- Dolphins make loud clicking sounds to knock out any small fish in range. Then they eat them.

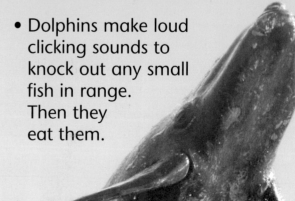

- A dolphin's extremely long jaws may contain as many as 250 pointy white teeth. That would keep a dentist busy!

- Mother dolphins have babysitters for their young. The dolphins' 'sisters' help the mother during the birth of her young. Sister dolphins also stay close to help with babysitting.

- Dolphins look like they are smiling all the time even if they are ill or injured. This is because they cannot move the muscles in their faces.

- A blue whale calf weighs two tonnes at birth. This is the same as two heavy horses!

- An adult blue whale's heart weighs as much as a small car.

- Female orcas have been known to live for up to 80 years.

- The deepest dive ever recorded for a bottlenose dolphin is about 300 metres. This was made by a dolphin trained by the US navy.

- Dolphin calves are born tail first so that they do not drown. Their mother quickly pushes them up to the surface of the water for their first breath.

- Dolphins have two stomachs – one for storing food and one for digesting it.

- A dolphin's skin is very sensitive and easily injured by rough surfaces – much like human skin.

- Dolphins can jump as high as 6 metres out of the water.

- Dolphins are not only found in the ocean but in rivers as well. Amazon river dolphins are born grey, but grow pink with age!

Whales and dolphins quiz

The answers to these questions can all be found by looking back through the book. See how many you get right. You can check your answers on page 56.

1) What is a baby dolphin called?
   A – Calf
   B – Pup
   C – Foal

2) The short-beaked common dolphin likes...
   A – Cold water
   B – Warm water
   C – Freezing water

3) How long can a male narwhal's tusk reach?
   A – 1 metre
   B – 2 metres
   C – 3 metres

4) Dolphins are...
   A – Fish
   B – Mammals
   C – Amphibians

5) What do cetaceans have instead of front legs?
   A – Flippers
   B – Arms
   C – Tusks

6) How does a dolphin breathe?
   A – Through its blowhole
   B – Through its nose
   C – Through its mouth

7) What do toothless whales have instead of teeth?
   A – Gums
   B – Baleen
   C – Fangs

8) What is another name for an orca?
   A – Fish
   B – Squid
   C – Killer whale

9) What stops a dolphin's eyes becoming sore from the salty water in the sea?
   A – Wax
   B – A thick, greasy liquid
   C – Blood

10) Dolphins can...
   A – Count
   B – Dance
   C – Understand simple sentences

11) What is it called when whales launch themselves out of the sea?
   A – Jumping
   B – Breaching
   C – Flying

12) Researchers can identify individual Risso's dolphins from...
   A – Their flippers
   B – The scars on their bodies
   C – Their eyes

Books to read

Explorers: Oceans and Seas by Stephen Savage, Kingfisher, 2010

The Best Book of Whales and Dolphins by Christiane Gunzi, Kingfisher, 2006

Weird Ocean by Kathryn Smith, Kingfisher, 2010

Whales and Dolphins by Susanna Davidson, Usborne Publishing Ltd, 2008

Wild World: Watching Dolphins in the Oceans by Elizabeth Miles, Heinemann Library, 2006

Places to visit

Birmingham Sealife Centre
www.sealife.co.uk
Experience the new four-dimensional cinema! Hear the power of the ocean's waves and surf the coast with the bottlenose dolphins. Learn about the Whale and Dolphin Conservation Society and find out what they are doing to try to prevent whaling. Observe other marine life such as sealions, otters and sea horses.

New Quay, Ceredigion, Wales
www.dolphincareuk.org
Visit New Quay and you may even spot dolphins in the wild! There are boat trips that take you in search of these wonderful animals. You might even spot a sealion on your travels!

The Natural History Museum, London
www.nhm.ac.uk
Learn about life in the sea and how whales and dolphins become stranded on the shores. Look at the awesome life-size model of a blue whale in the mammal gallery.

Websites

www.kids.nationalgeographic.com
Learn about bottlenose dolphins, orcas and whales with facts, photos, videos and games to play.

www.nhm.ac.uk
With a section just for children there are games to play, pictures and videos to look at. You can also learn about people who study whales and dolphins as their career.

www.dolphins-world.com
Learn about dolphin and whales with colouring pages, three-dimensional puzzles and pictures helping you to learn about these interesting animals.

Whales and dolphins
quiz answers

1) A	7) B
2) B	8) C
3) C	9) B
4) B	10) C
5) A	11) B
6) A	12) B